I0530373

THERIANTHROPIC DREAMS

NIGHTEYES DAYSPRING

DANCING JACKAL BOOKS

Therianthropic Dreams

Copyright © 2024 NightEyes DaySpring

All rights reserved. No part of this publication may be reproduced or used in any manner without the prior written permission of the copyright owner, except for the use of brief quotations in a book review.

First Edition Paperback, 2024

ISBN 978-1-957364-07-0 (paperback)
ISBN 978-1-957364-08-7 (e-book)

Dancing Jackal Books
Tallahassee, FL
www.dancingjackalbooks.com

Cover illustrated by Kippycube

For Dwale and Kiri, both of whom are sorely missed.
I wish you both could hold this work in your paws.

Contents

Foreword

We all dream. I've dreamed for a long time of worlds far away and a wolf who is me, but not me. Since high school, I've been writing some of these dream threads down and shaping them into poems and stories. Until now, I've rarely attempted to do anything with the poetry I've produced.

While I wrote new material for this collection, the oldest poem in this collection dates from 1999, when I was in high school. The words woven on these pages stretch across years of my life like a scattering of leaves, some pulled from loose pieces of notebook paper, and others digital bits that waited for a decade or more to see print.

Together, they are dreams, both good and bad, and among those dreams, shaping the text, is a wolf who walks on two paws and speaks like a man who is both me and not me. For over twenty-five years I've had this vision in the back of my mind. All these years later, I'm still not sure why he's there, why he is me, but so much of myself, and so many of the words I've written, come from him.

NightEyes DaySpring, May 2024

The Dream-Self Never Vanishes

It's a phase, it's not real,
but sometimes, it is.
Sometimes I feel my ears flick,
sometimes I feel my tail wag,
and I wonder, is it phase?
Is it imagination and a dream, or is it more?
Can I even tell that anymore?
Lying in bed, tired after a long day,
my feet and hands aching,
feeling like paws with pads,
that's just exhaustion, I think.
The urge to run after first watching that movie,
where the girl became a wolf while she sleeps,
that didn't go away all night—
I only laid in bed for hours,
desperately wanting to be one of those wolves in that movie.
It's a phase, isn't it?
The subtle way I perk up on well-lit nights,
wanting to go out and prowl—
it's not real, it's just a dream,
just the mind of a child, the mind of a teenager lost.
The fact I have dreamed about this for decades now…
perhaps it is a psychosis, perhaps just a fascination,
perhaps…a dream unlived,
or perhaps it's something more.
The urge to be what I'm not never goes away.
If this isn't who I really am,
why doesn't the dream ever end?
Does this dream show me the magic deep inside myself,
that I would unlock,
if the change would ever come?
I don't know anymore,
but I'm pretty sure it's not a phase.

Forward Into the Night

The dawn is too far away,
but the time has come. The time is now.
Find your courage,
forward into the night!

Let it swallow you whole,
let it blind you, let it smother you,
but stand strong, stride forward,
and hold your fear in check.

Just like the light, the dark is always there calling,
and fear will always be there, but do you fold?
Or do you put your paws forward, no matter how high your hackles get?
Come, forward into the night.

Forward into the despair. Forward on alone.
Forward for those not brave enough,
for those no longer capable and those who cannot take the risk,
for someone has to lead.

You said you were the one, the fearless, the brave,
and now the night is here, can you meet it?
Can you stand the darkness, and the blindness it brings,
and the way it gets into your fur?

Do you answer?
Can you reach the other side?
Can you step forward and open your senses to the night,
and keep your fear in check?

Can you be brave?
Can you be the wolf you said you were?
The night waits, O he who wants to see.
The darkness calls.

Prayer to Phoenix

O great bird of fire, and rebirth,
master of your own death, and child of the stars,
we call upon you to grant us your powers,
to let us soar through the sky,
so that we may see that world like you,
and to know the world as you do,
with its everchanging sands,
to realize that as mortal we may be,
we can be reborn out of the ashes,
of the lives we lead.

We ask that you only lift us up—
and let us see the world from an untainted view,
to know and learn from your age-old wisdom,
and help us see the cycles in the world around us.

Soulchange

The quiet time of night is when the wolf wants to run,
free to frolic,
under a sea of stars,
that reaches down into the well of myself.

Dawn brings the annihilation of dreams,
the world of mankind calls with its alarms,
with its machines to swallow us all.
Madness for paychecks to live without the joys of nature,
to live protected from the night.

My fur itches…

The human walks ahead,
the wolf runs forward,
into a world of endless trees and cool mist.
The forest swallows all,
and on the loam of a thousand years I shall sleep,
among the pines, at peace with myself.

My mind spins…
And the earth falls away—
Dawn once again brings the annihilation of dreams,
and I'm once again in the storm of reality.
The machinations of the modern world all around,
keeping me safe from the night,
in a dreamless reality.

My fur itches…
My tail trails behind me…
Give me the change,
footpaws and handpaws flexing—

Yet, these are things I don't have,
not in the annihilation of dreams that is reality.
I float in a darkness that is someone else's five-year plan,
whispered to their manager in their annual review,
a job and a paycheck,
and no joys of endless woods.

I can only scratch at the itches in my dreams,
as it all falls away in the dawn,
leaving me with the ache in my soul that never changes.

Call Down the Wind

Call down the wind—
the great traveler of our world—
let it pick you up and carry you.
Let it sweep across the cities,
blowing away the dust and grime.
Let it come to you,
as it journeys onward—
Listen to the words it whispers.
Hear its stories, and heed its wisdom,
for the wind speaks softly,
and rarely repeats itself.

Ink on Paws

The words come, and so I write.
The night turns and the dawn is distant, as I tap out my soul,
my dreams, my ideas, dripping down the page—
I hope they make sense.

In the dark, I write because I must,
digital black ink for the future.
Words to shape, words to revise,
stories to tell.

Dark blocks of ink curling into words,
shaped by my paws, shaped by my fears,
in the quiet of the night, in the center of myself,
visions of other worlds upon the page.

The dream, the nightmare, the everything I have become,
the determination to be more, the determination to be steel,
pages of text, words for the dead gods I dream about,
all shaped by my paws.

Lines of pencil across pages, sketchbooks with doodles,
ink blots on paper, let it all come!
Let it be, let it create, let it dream, let it spin upon the page!
Take my paw and plunge into this with me.

Hear my song, hear my voice, hear my pain!
Feel it all, and make it real, make it become, make it more,
as I chase myself across the page to make the ink sing,
a thousand voices for the paper to feel.

Everything becomes more, everything becomes ink,
for if I don't write these words who will?
No one else can be me, nor should they ever try to be...
because only I know these songs.

There's nothing special about that, just my personal madness,
just a mind turning in the bottom of a coffee cup,
and words to write and ink to make sing—
ink to make howl with my paws.

Words for tomorrow, words for today,
lines for projects yet realized,
for goals yet created, for thoughts to be recorded,
for futures to be, as messy as they might be.

For the people tomorrow who might read this, for the wolf today,
for the dawn yesterday I remember, let the words come.
Let the words flow, and let my paws shape these ideas.
May the ink bear record, and may I write well.

May the lines become shapes, and the ideas become stories,
let the trail of my thoughts bear witness,
let the dreams carry us forward to better.
May the ink live, alive with my ideas.

Two Sets of Eyes to See

Together, human and wolf,
we have walked the road of life.
We stepped lightly upon the road—
intertwined as one,
you and I have had the eyes to see,
and the ears to hear,
the whispered strains of truth.
Yet I am left grasping for straws,
in a field of sticks.

Chasing My Tail

Someday, I'll reach the end.
Someday, I'll stop dancing,
and with a sigh I will breathe my last breath.
The darkness will come, and I shall finally rest,
in the earth from which I came.
I will no longer be chasing my tail around in circles.
The dance I came here to perform will be over,
and as the curtain comes down,
I shall rest in the silence, where everyone goes.
But I'm not ready to go, not ready to pass on.
I refuse to stop dancing, stop fighting—
I plan to keep living till they yank me off the stage.
I refuse to simply wait for the end,
not when there is so much to do.
even if I trip and fall to the floor,
I will stumble back to my feet, and keep going,
even if chasing my tail is all I seem to be doing.
Even if I seem to keep going around in circles,
I'm going to keep on dancing.

The Last Time I Saw You
Lament for Dwale

It was in a cool northwest October where I first met you,
and it was in a warm southeast May where I last saw you.
Among the bustle of thousands of furs, we sat down as we planned,
and we talked about worldbuilding, about dreams, to a room full of people.
There's no record of this now except for our notes, a little over two years later,
and an entire pandemic between us, but I knew, when it was over,
and we returned to Atlanta, I was going to see you again in a room,
and we'd both be talking to a crowd about something—
and then you were gone.

Maybe it's my fault we weren't closer, but you touched so many people—
who was I to demand all your attention?
I wish I had said more, but I know I at least said something,
and I was so happy when I had a reason to send you a private message,
a week before you were gone, to ask a question of you—
now I only have what you told me and what you wrote to look back at.

There are still things I didn't ask I wanted to know,
words to seek your advice on, that I should have asked about—
but then I never thought you would be done so soon.
I don't understand what happened, but back when I saw you last,
when I walked out of the room, you were pleased about the panel.
It had gone well, you were happy, and you were smiling,
as you thanked me for asking you to do this with me,
before we were both on to our next things, as so many before us,
through the cavernous spine of Atlanta.

Race the Dawn

Paws down on the ground,
tongue rolling out, the wind brushes your fur.
The moon calls. The night sings.
Run, run for all you can—
howl to the darkness—
for you live anew.

Wood smoke tickles your nose,
as a bonfire lights up the dark.
Slap the earth with your footpaws.
Feel your claws dig down into it and spring up as you spin.
Dance to the beat of the drums,
and swing your tail around and laugh as you feel alive.

Ears flick and you smile with all your fangs—
not in threat, but in joy.
Feel the gentle touch of moonlight upon you,
smile and lean forward and gently caress your love,
for tonight you are, and tomorrow who knows,
but you can race the dawn tonight.

Paws on the ground, or heart in the sky,
the stars shine for you, and you won't let it go,
not now, not while you can be yourself and be free,
not while you still have life yet to live,
for all of you lives in this night,
and joyous you shall be.

Celebration of Spring

With a quick lupine stretch,
the hunter is off through the woods.
With ease, I break off into a run—
Ground flies by, under my paws.
As I run in the cool night air,
the northern forest is filled with song,
at the turning of the earth.
The forest is boundless,
with its sweeping hillsides,
and lush riverbanks.
I stalk under the moon,
hunting a small meal to abate my hunger.
During the day, I play in the clear blue waters,
fur drying in the warm lazy afternoon sunshine,
and I revel in my existence.
I celebrate in the circle of life.
I run and howl in tune with the song,
and there is beauty in this simple life.

Lost at Home

And so I came down finally,
and I arrived at my destination,
in the last hour of the day,
as the sun dips down low, setting everything aflame.
Yet it was not the same place,
that I ran down the streets as a kid.
It is different now,
and I could feel the changes as I stepped outside,
for an evening stroll.
So many places gone—
so many filled with different people now—
so few left that I know—
the houses are all filled with strangers.
It has been so long,
that there are trees now where there shouldn't be.
But I've come back finally.
I will stay,
and with what little time is left me,
I will spend it here.
I have come home at last.

Soulmates

Early morning sunlight falls through the trees,
filtering into a small clearing, and sparkles on freshly fallen snow.
Golden light illuminates gray fur—
Side-by-side two wolves sleep.
The weariness from the night's hunt,
and the warmth from each other,
has lulled them to contentment.
Eyes are squinted shut against the morning sun,
while intertwined tails twitch together,
and hearts beat in tune,
their souls sharing the same dream.

What Dreams
Lament for Kiri

In the swirls of your dream light, the sky was bright.
In the shadows of loss, you stood strong.
When you spoke, even the stones called back to you,
the earth echoing with your wisdom.

What dreams did you bring us?
What truths did you seek in the pages of ink you gave us?
Dreams of tomorrow, dreams of better,
they slipped out onto the paper under your paws.

How far you journeyed from where I knew you,
so wise you became and how greatly you ached,
and yet even in your lows,
you still stood up, when someone needed to.

I blink and there you are, standing bright in the dream,
the light swirling around you,
the fire unquenched.

So much more you wanted to teach us…
So much more you were going to be…

Yet before my eyes, the light twists and nothing remains.
When I cry out, you no longer answer.

Dhole sister, what dreams do you see?
What is there you saw you haven't yet told us?

Why must you leave so soon?

Seeing Yourself in Ink

The world is endless,
stretching to the limit of your imagination,
a realm of seas, hills, and plains,
where the sun sets,
and the moon rises into the starry sky.

It is cold and the wind blows,
trying to steal the warmth,
my fur provides.
I found shelter here in the brush last night,
but the wind was not so strong then.
I yearn for the warmth of summer—
to feel the sun's heat,
but now I am cold and hungry.
My stomach growls—
I will hunt when the blizzard breaks.
I will live because I want to.

The dreamland is vast.
A gigantic plane of thoughts—
a universe unto itself...

I put down the book I was reading.
and I don't see what is across the room—
my mind is still lost in the book's words.
I fetch a drink for I did not know I was thirsty,
before I pick up my book to read some more.

A million flames flickering
dancing across the world stage
souls burning bright,
all upon these pages.
How I long to be there with it.

Swiftly Running Shadows

With my paws barely disturbing the leaf litter,
I run with my wolf brothers and sisters.
Our tails flying behind us,
jumping over logs and splashing through streams,
we run silently through the deepening shadows of dusk,
and when the full moon rises,
we will break our silence with a howl of love.

Fragments of a Song

The beats course through you and into you,
your body undulates to the blissful noise,
the rhythm of the club music feels eternal,
and yet it changes all the time—
like the shore reshaped by the sea,
and even in the middle of a hundred swaying bodies,
entranced in the dark like you,
you can still feel alone.

Urges

I want to be touched in ways that make people blush...
it's only natural, but there is a little hitch—
I much prefer that be another guy,
same as me.
I never said I was shy about it,
just discreet—
I never would have written all those stories if I was shy.
Ruffle my fur, and watch me wag,
there is no shame in being gay.
I don't care what those bigots think.
I only wish I found my confidence sooner.
It's easier when you know who you are,
the way you smile, the way you touch and love,
it flows freely then.

The Goodbye Parties

It starts simple, it starts quietly.
Oh you're moving? Good for you!
And then they are gone.

You have them over, and you smile,
you drink, you laugh, and in the morning—
the moving van leaves...

There's always someone else at first,
someone else to join your social circle,
but slowly it starts to dwindle.

More leave, more go, and you're still behind,
you're still here waiting, thinking it won't be that bad—
hoping it won't be at least...

And one day, things change,
there are less of you, and yet you've never been a bigger problem—
at least to them.

The parties become more frequent,
now people aren't just leaving for better jobs,
they're leaving because they're scared.

They're leaving because they need to get out, but you're still here,
you're still hosting the parties,
and you wonder, when you go—

But you're brave, and you stay,
or maybe you can't afford it.
Maybe you're too damn stubborn to go.

And maybe one day they come for you,
and they slip that rope around your neck and pull and there you are—
hanging because of who you are and who you love—

Wait, oh, you're moving? Good for you!
Sorry I was lost there for a moment thinking,
wondering what happens next…

No, I wasn't crying, was I?
Sorry, so proud of you, so happy but also missing you—
and so very tired.

Oh yes, I heard about the mechanics just out of town,
with their sign and their hate, and maybe some rope…
but I'll be fine.

You'll be fine…
it will be fine…
and I'll be here, for now.

Something For the One I Love

I wake in the night,
and roll over.
I squeeze my eyes shut and listen,
and while sounds do reach my ears,
I do not hear what I want to,
and while my sheets keep me warm—
with me feeling nice and secure under them—
you are not here with me.
That little, gentle ache of loneliness—
I feel all the time is there,
because we must still be apart.

Yet I know I shall hold you in my arms again,
someday down the road,
and I know soon in the future,
when I wake at night, I will feel you there beside me.
I still love you and miss you.

Upon these gentle thoughts,
I drift back to sleep-
to dream of you,
and how happy we will be.

Fangs & Dirt

I - Dawn

The night guides us with its mysteries,
while the day touches us with its warmth.
Dawn is the moment of beginning, the moment of hope,
and here in the light of dawn, I see what must come.
I breathe for I must,
I feel because I can.
Foolish things perhaps to do in this world,
signs of the living,
but are we really living?
I don't know.
You tell me.

It doesn't matter if you don't know.

II - Naïveté

Winds that could kill swirl around me.
Winds that nibble at the bones.
Change that comes uninvited.
The slashing of time, the wrath of the present—
wounds that don't want to heal,
no matter how hard you treat them,
the claw marks growing old.
Watch for the carnivorous wind,
lest it catch you unaware,
because it always comes when you don't want it—
that's just the way things are.

III - Reality

I don't care if they pin me down and clamp fangs around my neck,
they'll have to squeeze everything out,
before I let go.
Someone must bear witness.
Someone must speak.
It doesn't have to be me, it shouldn't be me,
but I'm still here.
Even as I close my eyes and the vice-like jaws,
close around me,
threatening to break me…
As I struggle against formless mass,
feebly digging my dull claws in and scrabbling,
life desperately trying to hang on…

My eyes plead for your help…
A paw, a hand, a lifeline.
Anything really…
Nothing?

I should remember that time passes silently.

IV - Dirt

The dirt doesn't care—
it soaks up everything we give it,
every tear and drop of blood.
It bears silent witness to our struggles.
It catches us when we fall…
It holds us when we die, and it grows our crops,
it brings us our success and our death,
and it asks for nothing in return,
just that we honor our sacrifices.

The stains of who I am I leave upon it,
the alarm that comes no matter how tired I am,
a bed of dirt is all I get.

V - Circling

I stand again, and again the form comes,
but now I have learned.
Now I dodge—
the nameless mass can only catch me on the shoulder,
and it has to tire me out,
my blood upon the dirt, before it can make me yield,
before it can try and break me again.
Endlessly circling, I seek an advantage,
and each of my thrusts is rebuffed,
but at least now I'm only on the ground when I'm tired.

VI - Fangs

Time, you are cruel.
You wish to make each of us what we hate,
you try and break those of us who won't yield with your endless assault,
and yet I'm still here—
Not yet, you endless bastard!
Not today, and not tomorrow.
You made me grow these fangs,
you made me grow this fur.
You cut me so many times,
and yet here I am, still pushing,
still stepping up.

VII - Hope

The trees will bear witness, because they always do,
the wind will come like it always does,
the storm never relents, and yet...
if we can take some of the fight out if it,
we can make it easier for the next person,
we can make it kinder.
We can make it better.

Dawn comes every day.

Coffee Wolf

The black liquid of my life,
the chalice of molten joy,
O please my friend, wake my mind,
bring me a jolt that travels down my spine,
and into my paws and my tail.
Lend me your strength,
even if the buzz is fleeting.
Let me be more,
let me find joy, in this morning light.
May my ears perk in your glory,
and may my voice be strong this day.

Falling on Rainy Nights

And they say, that time heals everything—
I say time erases everything,
and we just forget where we hurt.
We simply forget why.

Have you ever noticed,
how the streetlights reflect down rain swept streets,
in the darkness of a rainy night,
beautiful, yet cold and wet?
The water that falls upon the streets,
washes down the road, running somewhere else.

The wind blows cold on those nights,
pushing the dampness into you.
Weather like that can be healing,
in that it makes you appreciate the sunshine,
and gives you a reason to curl up with a cup of tea,
and a book, reading to the patter on the roof.

Yet as the rain drops fall from the sky,
like the tears of the estranged,
too many of us don't let this weather,
wash through our souls, cleansing them—
instead, we watch TV, and don't realize,
what's going on outside.
The constant roar of the commercials,
wipes out the sounds of the rain.

We simply forgot about the warm chair,
the tea, and the book,
and lie on the couch,
watching those flickering images,
and we wonder why,
we never get around to reading anymore.

But the wind, the rain,
they're still going to come anyway,
and time will keep going on,
making us forget the little things,
like the aches and the pain.

The Skald's Plea

Put another log on the fire and pour me a mug of something fine,
and I'll tell you a story as I get the chill out of my fur.
I've crossed mountains and rivers to spin tales,
I've been in halls great and small trading my words for coin,
traveling further than the old bards ever did.

I've seen lakes clear and clean, and deserts hot and dry,
I've treaded miles unto miles to get here,
I've called out to the gods themselves and listened to the ripples,
and all for some coin to bring my words to the needy—
so listen and spare me your ear.

And let me tell you of my journeys and what I've seen,
let me tell you where the waves meet the sky and about the songs that don't end,
about the jackal who has swallowed millions,
and the dream light of futures lost, and futures gained,
all for my keep tonight.

For I am a skald, even if my words are not sung or inked in iron,
and I never thought I'd travel as far as the fox, but here I am,
your quirked ear wondering,
your heart yearning for warmth in this cold, dying world,
for I am a skald and I have stories still to share with you.

And perhaps if my words please you, you will give me a few coppers,
and a little piece of roast for my belly,
to help me stave off the cold on the road, as I journey on,
bringing my parchment and my stories with me,
to those who need the warmth only a good story can bring.

Eulogy

Like the pawprint trails of a wolf,
my words stretch behind me.

From an uncertain world, I go to an uncertain future,
but I follow in the path of those before me,
and in their braving of this journey,
so shall I.

I will be as brave as I can be.

May the ink flow.

About the Author

NightEyes DaySpring is a known troublemaker who is rumored to have a penchant for coffee and an interest in dead, ancient civilizations. He has been writing furry fiction for over twenty years. His work has appeared in various anthologies, including *Werewolves vs. Fascism*, *Heat*, and *FANG*. He also has contributed multiple stories to The Voice of Dog podcast, and he recently published his first novel, *Scars of the Golden Dancer*. He also has published two short story collections, *Knotty Works* and *Gnoll Tales*. Currently, NightEyes resides in Florida with his fiancé, where in his spare time he masquerades as an IT professional, plays board games, and doodles.

Visit his website, *nighteyes-dayspring.com*, for more about his writing, or find out where he is on social media at *nighteyes.carrd.co*.

www.ingramcontent.com/pod-product-compliance
Lightning Source LLC
Chambersburg PA
CBHW031240120626
46545CB00003B/1217